BATTLE OF VERDUN

A BRIEF HISTORY FROM BEGINNING TO END

HISTORY HUB

Bonus Downloads

*Get Free Books with **<u>Any Purchase</u>** History Shorts*

Every purchase comes with a FREE download!

Battle of Verdun

A Brief History from Beginning to the End

History Shorts

CONTENTS

Chapter One
Introduction

The Battle of Verdun is infamous for being the longest battle fought during World War I. It was also one of the bloodiest battles, claiming more than 700,000 victims. The battle was fought between France and Germany from February 21 to December 18, 1916. As a result of the war, the landscape surrounding the city of Verdun was completely transformed and a total of nine villages were utterly obliterated. The battle became symbolic of the brutality of war and the hallmark of French determination and self-sacrifice. The Battle of Verdun was a turning point in the war by halting the German advance and causing heavy losses to the Central forces. The loss of the Battle of Verdun delivered a crushing blow to the morale of the German forces, which ultimately impacted the outcome of the war. The Battle of Verdun was planned by German General Erich von Falkenhayn, who wanted to weaken the French army by causing heavy casualties. He believed that the British army, combined with the French army, could severely impact the outcome of the war. The other allies of the British were the Italian and the Russian armies. By then Russia had already been immobilized, and Italy was unlikely to cause any serious threat to the Central powers. That left out France and eliminating the French army would create an advantage for the Germans. Through the battle at Verdun, Falkenhayn wanted to "bleed France white."

Verdun was selected for the offensive due to its historical and sentimental value. Verdun was protected by a series of forts, whose history could be traced to the Middle Ages, and the loss of such a citadel was likely to cause a tremendous blow to the French morale. General Falkenhayn believed that capturing the forts of Verdun would trigger a sense of humiliation in the French army, and they would throw every man into its defense. Also, capturing the forts would give the Germans the benefit of height from which they could cause maximum damage to the French army.

At the initial stages of the war, the German offensive was very successful. They quickly advanced towards the fortress, preceded by heavy artillery firing, making the French army suffer heavy casualties in the first few days of the war. The Germans quickly captured fort Douaumont, the largest and the highest fort around Verdun, and turned it into the dumping ground for the German army. Meanwhile, the French counter attacks during the initial stages of the battle were mostly in vain, as the French army was initially disorganized and totally unprepared for the attack. The intelligence reports were dismissed by the high command, and a lot of troops and war supplies had been moved out of Verdun before the attack. By the time the French army understood the seriousness of the situation and started their battle preparations, it was already too late. The Germans were able to advance in the initial stages of the war with very little resistance.

Things changed significantly when the command of the French second army was given to General Philippe Pétain who reorganized troops to intensify the defense around the Meuse River. He brought in large reinforcements and introduced a noria (rotation) system to make sure the troops do not suffer from exhaustion. His efforts earned him the title "The Lion of Verdun." During the battle, he was promoted to Commander of Army Group Centre, leaving the charge of the second army to General Robert Nivelle, who was an excellent strategist himself. General Nivelle was also a spendthrift when it came to the lives of his men, which earned him the title "The Butcher." After months of devastating artillery firing, attacks by flamethrowers, trench warfare, and several casualties on both sides, the French took back the land and the fortresses that were captured by the Germans and pushed them to the starting line. The battle lasted for 302 days.

The Battle of Verdun became a symbol of the horrors of trench warfare and the destructiveness of war. It brought the armies of both sides to the brink of collapse. Several French villages were completely destroyed and remain uninhabitable to this date.

Chapter Two
World War I - A brief background

World War I, also known as the Great War or the First World War was one of the most significant events of the 20th century. The war raged from 1914 to 1918 and caused massive destruction and unprecedented loss of life and limb. Russia, the United States, the Middle East, and most of the European nations participated in the war. The participants were divided into two opposing groups: the Central Powers, and the Allied forces.

<u>Causes:</u>

On June 28, 1914, Archduke Franz Ferdinand of Austria, the heir apparent to the Austro-Hungarian throne was assassinated in Bosnia, along with his wife Sophie. The assailants were part of a movement called "Young Bosnia," which was fighting against Austrian rule in Bosnia. The primary assailant was a young Bosnian Serb named Gavrilo Princip, who was trained by the Serbian outfit known as the "Black Hand." The assassination outraged Austria-Hungary and gave them the perfect opportunity to launch hostilities against Serbia. Following Austria's declaration of war against Serbia, Russia got involved in support of Serbia.

Germany, on seeing Russia's involvement, declared war on Russia, which led to France being drawn in against Germany and Austria. Great Britain, being an ally of France, declared war on Germany. Initially, Italy had decided to remain neutral in the war despite being a partner in the Triple Alliance with Germany and Austria-Hungary. However, strong anti-Austria sentiments in the general public and political instability in the country led to Italy joining the war on the side of the Allied forces. Joining the war was seen as a means to unify the nation and invoke nationalist sentiments in Italy. Meanwhile over in Asia, Japan entered the war in 1914 as a means to extend its influence over China and the Pacific.

The United States, at this point, decided to take a neutral stance and not participate in the war. However, Germany embarked on a mission to isolate Britain and started sinking American merchant ships that entered the war zone around the British Isles, causing heavy casualties. Ultimately in April 1917, the United States entered the Great War by issuing a declaration of war against Germany.

The Central Powers:

The Central Powers, also known as the Quadruple Alliance consisted of Germany, Austria-Hungary, Bulgaria, and the Ottoman Empire. Apart from these nations, New Guinea and East Africa, which were both German colonies at the time, also fought on the Central Powers' side. Later, Finland, Azerbaijan, and Lithuania joined the Central Powers in 1918, after the collapse of the Russian Empire.

The term "Central Powers" was coined due to the location of the countries comprising it. All four of them were located between the Russian Empire on the eastern side and France and the UK on the west. The Central Powers were defeated by the Allied forces in the First World War, and Germany lost both its colonies by the end of the war.

<u>The Allied Forces:</u>

The Allied forces were a coalition of countries mainly consisting of France, the United Kingdom, Italy, Russia, the United States, and Japan. The colonies of these countries were also part of the Allied forces, like British India, the Indochinese Federation under the French and Japanese Korea. The Allied forces were subdivided into "Principal Allied" and "Associated Powers." The Principal Allied forces were Great Britain, France, and the Russian Empire, which were all part of a formal treaty called. The "Treaty of London" that was signed on September 5th, 1914. All the other nations, including the United States, that had come to be associated with one or more of the Principal Allies were classified as Associated Powers. The treaty signed at the Paris Peace Conference recognized 27 countries as "Allied and Associated powers." Apart from the United States, "Serbia, Belgium, Montenegro, Asir, Nejd and Hasa, Portugal, Romania, Hejaz, Panama, Cuba, Greece, China, Siam (now Thailand), Brazil, Armenia, Luxembourg, Guatemala, Nicaragua, Costa Rica, Haiti, Liberia, Bolivia, Ecuador, Uruguay and Honduras were all part of 'Associated Allies.'" The Allied forces defeated the Central Powers bringing an end to the Great War.

At the initial stages of the war, the German assault was very successful. By the end of 1914, Germany had captured most of France's domestic coalfields and inflicted heavy casualties. Throughout 1915 to 1917, Great Britain and France suffered more casualties than Germany. In February 1916, Germany attacked the French troops at Verdun. After Germany made initial gains in the Battle, the French counter attacks were successful in taking back lost territory. By the fall of 1918, the tides had turned in the favor of the Allied powers. On November 11, 1918, Germany signed an agreement of peace which caused the fighting to stop. The day came to be known as Armistice Day. The Treaty of Versailles, which was signed on

June 28, 1919, officially marked the end of the First World War. The main authors of the treaty were the leaders of France, England, Italy, and the United States. Germany suffered heavy losses and was brought to the brink of civil war. The war led to the end of imperialistic rule in Germany, and the end of the centuries-old Ottoman Empire.

Chapter Three
Verdun- History, and Strategic Importance

History of Verdun

Verdun is a city situated on the banks of the Meuse River—mostly on the left bank near the citadel—in the northeastern part of France. The city was officially called Verdun-sur-Meuse until 1970. The city derived its name from the Gaulish word Verodunum, meaning strong fort. From the early medieval period, Verdun has been well-known for its dDragées, or sugared almonds, which is a popular confectionery in France.

Verdun was founded by the Gauls, and since then was passed on among many short-lived empires from 400 AD to 1300 AD. The city became a part of the Holy Roman Empire in 1374 AD. The construction of a large citadel began around 1624, but it was only in 1670 that Sébastien Le Prestre de Vauban, a great military leader who worked under King Louis XIV, drew up an ambitious plan to fortify the entire city, much of which was built in the following years.

In 1792 AD, Verdun served as a battlefield for the Franco-Prussian war, which came to be known as the First Battle of Verdun. It was fought between the French revolutionaries and the Prussian army. The French were defeated and the Prussians captured the fortress of Verdun, thus gaining a clear path to Paris. Colonel Nicolas-Joseph Beaurepaire, who had commanded the defense of Verdun, was unable to bear the humiliation of this defeat and committed suicide. However, Verdun was soon abandoned by the Prussians after they lost to the French in the Battle of Valmy and were forced to retreat. In 1870, the Legion of Saxony, under the German military, laid siege to Verdun. Verdun put up a stronger defense this time but was defeated and forced to surrender. The Franco-Prussian war ended with France's defeat at the hands of a coalition of German states led by Prussia, resulting in the creation of a unified Germany. The Germans held Verdun till 1873. The defeat caused the French public to harbor deep resentment and demand for revenge against Germany, which manifested during World War I.

<u>Why Verdun?</u>

After the loss of Verdun to the Germans in 1870, the French heavily fortified the city to counterbalance any further attacks. By late 1915, France had proved itself to be a strong ally of the British Empire and one of the most formidable of the Allied powers. The German General Erich von Falkenhayn believed that weakening the French defenses would also weaken the British Empire whose real weapons were the French, Italian and Russian armies. By then, both Russian and Italian armies were rendered incapable of putting up a strong defense, and only France remained. General Falkenhayn wanted to wage war on France only to keep their armies occupied and cause heavy losses to the French side. He wanted to "bleed France white."

As a part of its strategy of war by attrition, Germany carefully selected the fortified city of Verdun for the attack for a number of reasons. They believed that the loss of the citadel of Verdun would cause a crushing blow to the morale of the French army. Also, capturing the high fortress would prove to be of immense strategic advantage for the Germans, from where they could launch heavy artillery warfare causing maximum damage to the French army. The fortress of Verdun also threatened the German communication lines and capturing it would be an added advantage to the Germans. Due to the strategic importance and the historic sentiment attached to Verdun, Falkenhayn strongly believed that France would defend Verdun to the last man.

<u>**Preparations for the Battle:**</u>

The German army emptied vast areas populated by French civilians, laid telephone cables stretching thousands of kilometers, and moved a huge amount of ammunition and ration to Verdun. Vast underground shelters and ten new rail lines with twenty stations were built by the Germans, and a total of 1,201 guns were sent to the Verdun front. By 1914, Verdun was already isolated on three sides by the 5th Army of the Germans, leaving only a light railway to carry bulk supplies to the French.

The French airmen were the first to detect German preparations for battle as early as January 1916. However, the French army initially dismissed these reports considering them a diversion. Later, on February 11, 1916, a French intelligence officer discovered German troops just outside of Verdun. Over the next 10 days, the French army sent thousands of men and war supplies to Verdun.

Chapter Four
Battle Strategies and Military advancements

<u>German Strategy and initial attack</u>

The German 5th Army divided the attack front into four areas: A, B, C, and D. The attack on Verdun was to begin on 12th February 1916, as per the original plan. The initial objective was to capture the Meuse Heights to secure a defensive position to repel the French attack. The initial attack was to begin in areas A to C, supported by grenade and flame throwers. The French trenches were to be occupied wherever possible. The German army stressed the accuracy of their firing on the French fortification. However, due to bad weather, the German attack was delayed until 7:15 am on the 21st of February 1916 when German artillery opened fire with 808 guns. The German army fired around 1,000,000 shells for ten hours, which concentrated mainly on the right bank of the river Meuse, towards the forts of Verdun, and was to be continued throughout the night. The German strategy was to create "relentless pressure" and lure in the maximum number of French troops to Verdun and thus cause heavy casualties to the French army. The firing was stopped mid-way on the same day as a ruse to lure out the surviving French soldiers, after which the German army specifically targeted them using stormtroopers and flamethrowers. The German artillery observation aircraft hovered in the sky to flush out the French survivors.

By 22nd February, the Germans had captured Bois des Caures, at the edge of the village of Flabas. The French army launched a counterattack but was defeated. In the following days, the Germans captured Beaumont-en-Verdunois, Bois des Fosses, and Bois des Caurières and started advancing toward Fort Douaumont.

French Strategy and counterattack

In 1915, a lot of supplies were diverted from Verdun for the Second Battle of Champagne. The Verdun fortresses were mainly occupied by maintenance crews and were left unguarded. The initial reports by intelligence officers were dismissed by the German commanders, owing to the lack of a strategic objective. The German attack had left Verdun isolated on three sides. The railway was rendered unusable due to heavy bombardment from the Germans. The French, therefore, relied on a fleet of more than 3,000 trucks to transport men and war supplies to the war front. Due to the logistical disadvantage and the initial delay in the preparations, the French suffered heavy losses in the initial stages of the battle.

By the end of the first day of battle, the German army had made significant gains by penetrating the French defense and occupying Bois d'Haumont. The French launched a counterattack the next day, but were defeated. By February 23rd, the villages of Brabant-sur-Meuse, Wavrille, and Samogneux were in German hands, after which the French army brought in heavy reinforcements. The Germans started their advancement towards Fort Douaumont.

Under the leadership of French commander Gen. Philippe Pétain, a fresh army was brought in on February 25th, with the sole objective of defending the right bank of river Meuse. The initial strategy was to place a large number of French troops on the left bank of the river Meuse to prevent the Germans from crossing the river. However, a change of French strategy left Fort Douaumont unguarded, which was captured by the Germans. Fort Douaumont was of immense strategic importance and its capture was a huge blow to the French army. The French defense strengthened in the next few days, and they were able to slow down

German advancement. The French air force was brought in to assist, and the communication lines were improved.

Important People

The Battle of Verdun was one of the most significant events of the First World War, in which several people played major roles. German General **Erich von Falkenhayn** was convinced that defeating the French army would weaken the British defenses considerably, thus creating a clear advantage for the Germans. Falkenhayn chose Verdun to launch the attack against the French due to the strategic importance and historical sentiments attached to it. The German army appointed none other than **Prince Wilhelm**, the Crown prince of Germany, as the local commander for the battle.

General **Joseph Joffre,** who was the commander-in-chief of the French army, drew heavy criticism for diverting war resources from Verdun to other parts of the country. He also drew flak for undermining the intelligence reports on the German attack on Verdun. The command of the French second army at Verdun was given to **General Philippe Pétain**. Fort Douaumont was captured by the German forces immediately after General Pétain took command. General Pétain then organized a more extensive defense in the fortified region of Verdun and ordered there to be no retreat. In May 1916, General Pétain was promoted to the command of Groupe d'armées du centre (GAC), leaving the command of the second army at Verdun to **General Robert Nivelle.**

Under General Nivelle, the French army began large-scale counterattacks. By June 1916, the German offensive at Verdun was reduced to reinforce the Somme front. General Nivelle seized this opportunity to launch a vicious attack on the Germans and recaptured most of the forts.

General Philippe Pétain was famously known as "The Lion of Verdun."

Pictured above are the World War I forts at Verdun and Douaumont,

France.

Chapter Five
First phase of Battle

<u>Commencement of Battle</u>

The German offensive commenced on 21st February, 7:15 am. The attack on Verdun was named" Operation Judgement." The German army started heavy bombardment on a front 40-km long, on the right bank of the Meuse River. The objective was to cause maximum damage to the forts of Verdun. The bombardment was stopped towards noon as a ruse to discover the surviving French soldiers, after which the German army specifically targeted them using stormtroopers and flamethrowers. The German artillery observation aircraft hovered in the sky to flush out the French survivors. At about 4:45 pm, the first German infantry attack was launched. Twenty-six super-heavy, long-range guns, up to 420 mm were used on the first day of the battle to fire at the fortified city, which caused a rumble so loud that it could be heard from a distance of 160km. The surviving French soldiers engaged in heavy firing with the Germans but were unable to cause much damage. The German army suffered only 600 casualties on the first day of the battle and had captured Bois d'Haumont.

22nd-24th February

By 22 February, German troops had advanced into French territory and captured Bois des Caures at the edge of the village of Flabas. A distinguished French Colonel Émile Driant was martyred during the attack. The French launched a counterattack at Bois des Caures on February 23rd but were unsuccessful in recapturing it. That same day, the villages of Brabant-sur-Meuse, Wavrille, and Samogneux fell into German hands and the village of Haumont had been razed by artillery fire. On February 24th, the Germans tried to advance from their position at Samogneux, but were met with heavy resistance from the French. However, the remaining German army captured Beaumont, the Bois des Fosses, and the Bois des Caurières and started advancing towards Fort Douaumont.

The fall of Fort Douaumont

Fort Douaumont was the largest and highest of all the forts at Verdun and was key to defending the city from German advances. While the Germans were rapidly advancing towards Fort Douaumont, the fort was mostly unguarded, manned only by a maintenance crew of 56 troops and a few gunners. Bad communication had left the occupants of the fort vulnerable and totally unprepared for the attack. On 25 February, around 10 German soldiers, led by Sergeant Felix Kunze approached the fort. The Germans were spotted in Douaumont by French gunners, but due to poor visibility, they were mistaken for French troops returning from a patrol. Upon reaching the fort, Sergeant Kunze and his men found the moat unoccupied, and even without French resistance, the troops were hesitant to enter the fort, fearing an ambush. Hence, Sergeant Kunze entered the fort alone, armed only with a rifle, and captured the French artillery team single-handedly. Another group of German troops, led by reserve-officer Lieutenant Eugen Radtke also entered the fort and captured a few more French defenders. Later, more German troops entered the fort and defeated and captured every single of the French defenders, without firing a single shot. The loss of Fort Douaumont, practically without a fight, was a crushing blow to the French morale and caused severe losses to the French army in the following days of the battle. After its capture, Douaumont became an operational base for German forces.

Chapter Six
Aftermath and change of command

<u>General Pétain assumes command</u>

The French army faced heavy losses in the first few days of the battle due to a lack of clear strategy and bad decisions. General Joseph Joffre was heavily criticized for undermining the reports of French intelligence officers about the attack on Verdun. Under General Joffre, the French General Staff decided in 1915 to partially disarm all the Verdun forts, a decision that would cost them heavily in the subsequent months. After failing to stop the German advance during the first two days of the battle, General Joffre was set aside in favor of General Philippe Pétain who took command at the same time Fort Douaumont was captured by the Germans.

General Pétain took command of the French Second Army on February 25th. After assuming command, General Pétain organized a more extensive defense around the fortified regions of Verdun. He ordered the remaining Verdun forts to be re-garrisoned, and a line of resistance was established to prevent the remaining forts from falling into German hands.

General Pétain greatly improved the communication system by linking new telephone lines. Under him, the French troops were able to resist the German attack on Douaumont village. At the end of the war, General Pétain came to be known as "The Lion of Verdun."

French reinforcements

The French army brought in heavy reinforcements, and all the forts surrounding Fort Douaumont were occupied, rearmed, and supplied to withstand an attack. The Second Army, under General Pétain, assumed charge of defending the right bank of river Meuse. General Pétain increased the volume of traffic, carrying men and ammunition to the battlefield. The narrow Bar-le-Duc to Verdun road later came to be known as the "Sacred Way." Around 4,000 trucks, 2,000 cars, 800 ambulances, 200 buses, and numerous vans passed along it.

27-29 February

After capturing Fort Douaumont, the German army could make very few advancements in the following days of the battle. Bad weather had turned the ground into a swamp rendering some of the German artillery unserviceable. Meanwhile, the French defenses had gotten stronger owing to massive reinforcements. The German army was also suffering from exhaustion and heavy casualties in Douaumont village. Heavy snowfall helped the French troops contain German advancement at Douaumont on 29th February. The German army tried to advance southwards but was countered by heavy artillery firing by the French, causing heavy casualties to the German side. The delay gave the French army an advantage to bring in more reinforcements to the west of the river Meuse, which was left practically unguarded earlier.

The muddy conditions had made it very difficult for the German army to move their artillery and other equipment, which kept getting stranded in the mud. The hard conditions at Verdun caused a serious dilemma for the German generals who struggled to decide between terminating the offensive and reinforcing it. The Germans set up a specialist artillery force to counter French artillery fire from the west bank, but this also failed to reduce German infantry casualties. The German 5th Army's request for more troops was refused by German General Falkenhayn who needed a reserve of troops to launch an offensive at a different location. However, on 29th February, the 5th Army managed to obtain two divisions to capture the heights on the west bank of river Meuse.

Are You Enjoying Reading?

As an independent publisher

with a tiny marketing budget

we rely on readers, like you.

If you're receiving help from this book,

would you please take a moment to write a brief review?

We really appreciate it.

Chapter Seven
Second Phase of Battle

<u>March 4th to April 9th</u>

On March 4th, Douaumont village was captured by the Germans, which left the town destroyed. They expanded their scope of attacks on the west bank of Meuse and occupied Côte de l'Oie. The Germans then attacked Avocourt and Côte 304 on March 9, reducing the Côte 304 from a height of 304m to 300m. On March 10, the Germans captured the Bois de Cumières, clearing the way for an attack on one of the strongholds of the French, a hill known as Le Mort Homme. The lower crest of Le Mort Homme fell to the Germans on March 14th. The highest crest could be captured neither by the French nor the Germans, and was declared "No man's land."

The battle was now raging on both banks of the Meuse River, and the Germans had achieved their goal of capturing the east bank of the river. However, the French guns along the east of river Meuse caused significant damage to the German army. From large operations, they changed to narrow-front attacks with clear and limited objectives.

The Germans had to change strategy in order to hold on to the gains of the first phase. On March 8, the Germans captured the area surrounding Hardaumont on the right bank. For the next 10 days, they engaged in battle with French forces on the fort and the village of Vaux, the results of which were inconclusive and caused heavy casualties on both sides. On 20th March, the Germans attacked Bois d'Avocourt and Bois de Malancourt, and took control of them easily. The German commander ordered a pause in the attack to consolidate their gains and to plan a bigger attack the next day. On 22nd March, the Germans attacked Termite Hill near Côte 304 but were defeated by French artillery firing. This ended the German advancement on the right bank.

The Germans brought in fresh reinforcements and resumed attacks on the left bank, but they lacked the advantage of surprise. By the end of March, the Germans had faced heavy losses and limited gains. By April 8th, while the French army had lost all their strongholds on the left bank of the river and their former front line, the French artillery caused severe casualties to the German side and cut off their supplies. General Falkenhayn wanted to end the offensive. However, on April 9th, Germany launched a large-scale attack on both banks of the river on the orders of Crown Prince Wilhelm against the advice of General Falkenhayn.

Change of Commanding officers

The battle had reached a stalemate by the end of April, with both sides failing to make any significant gains. The German offensive on both banks of the river was inconclusive. Both sides changed their commanding officers. General Pétain was promoted to commander of Army Group Centre, leaving the charge of the 2nd Army to General Robert Georges Nivelle. The German command divided the field of battle into two parts, with Gen. Ewald von Lochow taking over from Gen. Bruno von Mudra on the right bank, while Gen. Max von Gallwitz commanded the left bank.

Preparations for Battle of Somme

The preparations for the upcoming Battle of Somme exerted pressure on both sides to bring the Battle of Verdun to a conclusive end.

To this day, the remains of Fort Douaumont at Verdun can still be visited.

Illustrated above is a Wounded soldier being carried away at Verdun.

Chapter Eight
Third Phase of the Battle

<u>Germans change tactics</u>

By the end of April, the Germans were facing heavy casualties from continuous artillery fire. Their communication lines and reserve positions were also heavily compromised. The German army found it very difficult to hold defensive positions, as those had been destroyed by French bombarding earlier, leaving very little cover. The objective of the German army was now to look for safer defensive positions. General Falkenhayn changed German defensive tactics to a dispersed defense with the second line to be held as a main line of resistance. The infantry was given limited areas to defend, and machine guns were set up with overlapping fields of fire. However, these tactics had very little impact, and the German army continued to face heavy casualties from artillery firing. From 4th to 24th May, the Germans attacked the west bank of the river Meuse and captured the north slope of Côte 304, successfully repelling two French counterattacks in early May.

French Counterattack

In May, General Nivelle, the new commander of the French Second Army started planning the recapture of Fort Douaumont. The charge was to be led by General Charles Mangin, commander of the 5th Division. On 8th May, a cooking fire caused a massive explosion in the fort by detonating grenades, killing hundreds of German soldiers and injuring many more. The ones trying to escape the fire were mistaken for French troops and fired upon. The incident caused great damage to the German army.

The French army managed to occupy the western end of the fort for 2 days but was repelled by heavy artillery firing by the Germans. Fort Douaumont had become a shelter for German troops and a first aid center. The Germans aggressively defended the fort, as the loss of Fort Douaumont would cost them heavily. The French continued artillery firing on the fort, causing severe damage to it and obliterating many defensive positions. By 22nd May, the communication lines were severely hampered and food had run out. The Germans retaliated by intensifying artillery firing from their end causing severe casualties to the French army. The 129th Infantry Regiment of the French army reached the fort and got in through the west and south ends. They recaptured half of the fort in a few hours and called for reinforcements the next day. However, the German troops foiled the reinforcements and captured the French troops inside the fort. They were forced to surrender and taken captive by the Germans.

June

On June 1, Vaux and Thiaumont were attacked by German troops, with both positions captured by June 9. Both points were essential to the French line of defense, and they resisted the attack at the south of Thiaumont. On June 21, the Germans renewed their attack on the right bank of river Meuse and captured the towns of Fleury and Souville. However, the French troops were able to resist the capture of Froide Terre, which was a French stronghold. On June 27th, General Pétain put in all resources to hold the right bank of river Meuse.

Chapter Nine
Fourth Phase of the Battle

<u>German advance is halted</u>

The French recaptured Chapelle Sainte-Fine, halting the German advance. By then, the Germans became vulnerable to fire from three directions, and the supply of water to German infantry broke down. The French army continued their counterattack on Fleury, which changed hands several times from June to August. By June 24, the French artillery cut off the German front line from the rear. On June 25th, the German army suspended the attack. By the end of June, German casualties outnumbered those on the French side.

The upcoming Battle of Somme forced the German army to divert some of their artillery from Verdun to Somme. In July, the Germans attempted to capture Fort Souville, which was of strategic importance to both sides due to its heights overlooking Verdun. The Germans began bombardment with gas shells but were unable to cause much damage to the French troops who were equipped with gas masks. The counterattack by the French army forced the Germans to retreat. The Germans then went on the defensive and managed to repel another large attack by the French army.

August - September

On 1st August, the Germans made another attempt to capture Fort Souville. A bloody battle ensued for two weeks. By August 18th, the French army had been able to recover most of the territory that was lost in July and August. The German high command went through a massive change when Falkenhayn was replaced as Chief of the General Staff by Paul von Hindenburg. The town of Fleury was back in French hands, and a counterattack by the Germans failed.

Recapturing Fort Douaumont

The French army under Charles Mangin began an offensive to take back Verdun on October 21st. They began heavy-range artillery firing. Seven of the 22 divisions at Verdun were replaced by mid-October, and French infantry platoons were reorganized to contain sections of riflemen, grenadiers, and machine-gunners. They pounded the fort for two days with two long-range Saint-Chamond French railway guns, "Lorraine" and "Alsace." Charles Mangin created three infantry divisions to recapture Fort Douaumont, which began the offensive on 24th October 1916. More than 20 very heavy shells, each weighing 1 short ton, hit Fort Douaumont. One of them penetrated the lower level of the fort and exploded near a bunch of hand grenades, causing a massive fire. 679 German soldiers perished in this fire.

The three infantry divisions, the 38th Division led by General Guyot de Salins, 133rd Division led by General Fenelon F.G. Passaga, and 74th Division led by General Charles de Lardemelle, attacked the fort around 11:40 am on October 24. They slowly advanced towards the fort behind a barrage of artillery firing forcing the German infantry to take cover. The Germans had partially evacuated the fort by then, unable to bear the brunt of the artillery firing and destruction caused by the fire. The remaining German soldiers were easily defeated. The French army recaptured the fort on 24th October with almost zero resistance from the Germans, taking 6,000 German soldiers as prisoners and recovering fifteen machine guns.

Chapter Ten
Last Phase of the Battle

Recapturing Fort Vaux

Fort Vaux was one of the nineteen forts constructed to protect the city of Verdun. It was the second fort to be captured by the German, the first being Fort Douaumont. The French attempted to recapture Fort Vaux right after successfully capturing Fort Douaumont, but this plan was foiled by the Germans. A second attempt to recapture Fort Vaux was launched by the French soon after. The tactics employed in the operation were similar to those used at Fort Douaumont. Heavy artillery firing was used from the same French railway guns, "Lorraine" and "Alsace." They bombarded the fort for two weeks, forcing the German soldiers to evacuate it on November 2, 1916. The wireless messages of the Germans, announcing the evacuation were intercepted by the French, and a French infantry entered the fort immediately after with no resistance.

December

By November 5th, the French army had reached the front lines and operations were ceased until December. In December, General Pétain and

General Nivelle launched the second offensive at Verdun. The offensive was to start on November 29, as per the original plan, but was delayed due to bad weather. Five German divisions were still holding their defensive positions in and around Verdun. The operations were to be commanded by General Charles Mangin. He intended on taking back the whole of the former French line that had been lost to the Germans last February 24. The objective of the operation was to flush out German troops from their trenches, observation posts, and dugout entrances. Two of the German divisions were already understaffed, with only 3,000 men, as opposed to the normal 7,000.

Due to the delay in the original plan, the Germans caught wind of it, and the French lost the advantage of surprise. They also launched a violent attack to counter the French, capturing Hill 304. By December 9, the weather had cleared, and the French were ready to launch an offensive. Both armies engaged in artillery duels and tried to capture maximum ground, with assistance from the airforce of both countries.

End of Battle

On December 15, the French launched a large-scale attack to recapture the remaining territory from Germany. At 10 AM, four French divisions assailed the German lines, and recaptured the whole of Poivre Hill. German reinforcements were too late to arrive, as the artillery firing had severely hampered their communication and supply lines. The German defense collapsed, and 13,500 men of the 21,000 in the five front divisions were lost, either killed or captured by the French. The French army continued in their advancement and re-captured Vacherauville, Hardaumont, and Louvemont, which were lost to the Germans earlier in February. They also captured and destroyed 115 guns and took 9,000 German prisoners. The entire operation came to be known as the Battle of Louvemont. It was concluded on December 18, when the French recaptured Chambrettes where 11,000 German prisoners were taken captive. It officially marked the end of the Battle of Verdun.

The Douaumont Ossuary was built in 1932 to commemorate the unidentified martyrs of the Battle of Verdun.

Pictured above is a French artillery aircraft shot down.

Chapter Eleven
Casualties and After-effect

The Battle of Verdun, which lasted for 302 days, came to be known as the longest and the bloodiest battle of the First World War. Beginning as a brilliant German offensive, the battle ended as an offensive victory for the French, when they repelled the German forces from the French territory. However, it brought both armies to the brink of collapse. The Battle of Verdun claimed over 700,000 lives, leaving many others injured or captured. The French suffered around 377,231 casualties and the Germans around 337,000.

The German 5th Army commander and the commander of XIV Reserve Corps were sacked on December 16. The Germans suffered heavy casualties in the Battle of Verdun. These losses, combined with the casualties at the Battle of Somme created a manpower crisis in the German army. On the other hand, the Battle of Verdun became a symbol of the French determination and destructiveness of the war. The fortress around river Meuse held historic and sentimental values for the French, and its loss would have caused irreparable damage to the French morale. By repelling the Germans, the French not only saved their territory from falling into German hands but also established themselves as a formidable opponent in the war. However, the number of casualties suffered by the French drastically reduced the size of their army, so the British army had to take the lead for the remainder of the war.

The Battle completely transformed the landscape around the city of Verdun and caused irreparable damage to many villages and the surrounding fortress. Nine villages—Beaumont, Bezonvaux, Cumières, Douaumont, Fleury, Haumont, Louvemont, Ornes, and Vaux—were entirely destroyed. These villages were memorialized, and their existence is preserved to honor the martyrs of the war. The area around the Verdun ridge was rendered unfit for habitation due to tons of war ammunition being stuck in the soil. The area was declared a "Red Zone." Unexploded ammunition and bullet shells, many filled with arsenic, continue to be recovered from the area, and as per reports have retained their toxicity. The extensive use of flamethrowers, artillery, and poisonous gasses had a devastating impact on the war zone and created a "moon" landscape on Earth. By the end of the battle, the French had managed to repel the

Germans to the starting trenches, but they paid a terrible price trying to protect a piece of land that was basically strategically useless.

Douaumont Ossuary is a monument that was built in 1932 to commemorate the unidentified martyrs of the battle. The monument holds the remains of 150,000 unidentified French and German soldiers. The ones who survived the battle suffered the consequences for the rest of their lives. "Shell shock" and other mental health illnesses were common among the survivors. The battle was fought in a narrow stretch of land, in terrible conditions and bad weather. The soldiers who tried to escape were either court-martialled or executed upon being caught. The Battle of Verdun also brought to light the horrors of trench warfare.

The Douaumont Ossuary holds the remains of 150,000 unidentified French and German soldiers.

Chapter Twelve

Conclusion

The Battle of Verdun had devastating consequences for both sides, as can be expected from an offensive that was initiated solely to cause loss of lives. It represented perfectly well the havoc caused by war. With over 700,000 casualties and many more injured or captured, the battle brought both the French and German armies to the brink of collapse. After 10 months of battle, the French army was able to recapture the territory from the Germans and repel them to the starting line, but not without causing considerable damage to the landscape. Nine villages in France were completely destroyed. These villages were memorialized and their existence is preserved to honor the martyrs of the war. The Douaumont Ossuary, a monument completed in 1932, holds the remains of 150,000 unidentified French and German soldiers. The battle also resulted in a large number of troops taken in as prisoners of war, who had to endure horrible living conditions and torture in captivity. The area around the Verdun ridge was rendered unfit for habitation due to tons of war ammunition being stuck in the soil. With the area declared a "Red Zone," miners might be digging out toxic substances from the soil for centuries to come. The ones who survived the battle suffered the consequences for the rest of their lives. "Shell shock" and other mental health illnesses were common among the survivors. A French soldier trying to describe the horrors of the battle wrote in his diary:

"Humanity is mad. It must be mad to do what it is doing. What a massacre! What scenes of horror and carnage! I cannot find words to translate my impressions. Hell cannot be so terrible. Men are mad!"

On the other hand, the battle became a symbol of French determination and courage. The loss of Verdun would have been a crushing blow to the morale of the French army due to the historic and sentimental value it held. As predicted by the Germans, the French did defend Verdun to the last man, but under the strong leadership of General Pétain and General Nivelle, managed to turn the tides significantly in the last phase of the battle. The French army overcame bad weather and poor conditions to repel the German army, which was more organized and prepared at the start of the battle. The Battle of Verdun greatly impacted the number of French troops in the Battle of Somme. The number of casualties suffered by the French drastically reduced the size of their army, so the British army had to take the lead for the remainder of the war.

Verdun has since then become a representative memory of the First World War for the French. The fortresses around Verdun became the object of national pride. By the 1960s, the countries involved had decided to leave the animosity behind and re-establish Verdun as a symbol of peace between France and Germany. In the 1980s, Verdun stood as a "remembrance of common suffering."

Chapter Thirteen

Discussion Question

The Battle of Verdun is considered to be the longest and the bloodiest battle of the First World War. Who would you consider the main culprit of the battle? What were the conditions that contributed to prolonging the battle?

Discussion Question

The Germans originally adopted the strategy of the War of Attrition, which was to cause maximum casualties to the French army. However, halfway through they decided to launch a large-scale offensive around the Meuse River. Do you think this was a good strategy? Who was responsible for the change in strategy?

Discussion Question

The Germans had to continue their offensive on Verdun far longer than they had predicted. Do you think the Germans underestimate the French army? What was the biggest strength of the French army?

Discussion Question

General Pétain and General Nivelle, who commanded the French Second Army were hailed as national heroes after the battle. However, both of them were known to be harsh on their troops with very little regard for their lives. What do you think of their approach? Did their battle strategies cost more lives than the German attack?

Discussion Question

What do you think was the most significant outcome of the battle?

Did it contribute to the outcome of the First World War? How?

Discussion Question

The Battle of Verdun became a symbol of the horrors of trench warfare. What do you understand about trench warfare? What made trench warfare so devastating?

Discussion Question

In the initial days of the battle, the Germans were able to capture French territory with minimum resistance. The French army was highly disorganized and understaffed at the time. Who would you consider responsible for the initial losses the French suffered?

Discussion Question

The Battle of Verdun had disastrous consequences for both sides. How did the battle impact the lives of the residents of Verdun? Was Verdun and its residents treated merely as "collateral damage" by the warring nations?

Chapter Fourteen
Quiz Question

1. . **True or False:** The Germans attacked Verdun to take advantage of the fortresses around river Meuse. They wanted to use the citadel as a hideout. The city was of immense strategic importance to the Germans.

2. **True or False:** The French army predicted the attack on Verdun several months prior. They spent several days preparing and strategizing for the battle. Fort Douaumont was especially re-garrisoned to counter the German attack.

3. **True or False:** The Battle of Verdun was planned by German General Erich von Falkenhayn, who wanted to weaken the French army by causing heavy casualties. He believed that the British army, combined with the French army, could severely impact the outcome of the war. Through the battle at Verdun, Falkenhayn wanted to "bleed France white."

4. **True or False:** The French armies were able to repel the German attack in the first stage of the war. The German army suffered more casualties

than the French on the first day. The French army was able to counter the attack without any reinforcements.

5. **True or False:** The battle of Verdun lasted for 302 days. It was the longest battle of the First World War. The war ended when the French army was able to repel the German army from Verdun.

6. **True or False:** The attack on Verdun was to begin on 12th February 1916, as per the original plan, but was delayed due to bad weather. The battle was fought between France and Germany from February 21 to December 18, 1916. The French emerged victorious in the battle.

7. **True or False:** The Battle of Verdun had no significant effects on the landscape of the region. There was almost no damage to the villages. The residents went back to their old homes after the battle.

8. **True or False:** The Battle of Verdun claimed over 700,000 lives. The French suffered around 377,231 casualties and the Germans around 337,000. The Douaumont Ossuary was built in 1932 to commemorate the unidentified martyrs of the battle.

Quiz Answer

1. False. The Germans attacked Verdun to cause maximum casualties to the French army. Verdun was otherwise of no strategic importance to the Germans.

2. False. The French army was late in starting preparations for the battle.

3. True

4. False. The French army suffered more casualties than the Germans initially. It took the French 10 months to repel the Germans from Verdun.

5. True

6. True

7. False. Several villages were permanently destroyed and declared uninhabitable after the battle.

8. True

Bonus Downloads

*Get Free Books with **<u>Any Purchase</u>** History Shorts*

Every purchase comes with a FREE download!